The Heart of a Military Mom

Finding Joy in Your Journey

Army Mom Strong
and
Elaine Brye

The Heart of a Military Mom
HeartofaMilitaryMom.com

Cover photo by:

Tonya Brye of Brye Photography
BryePhotography.com

Photo Credits:

Tonya Brye
Eric Brye
Courtney Brye

Logo by:

Ben Dixon
Benjamin74.com

ISBN-13: 978-1545365069

ISBN-10: 1545365067

DEDICATION

In honor of my children who made me a military mom and my son's best friend, Major Sterling "Stranger" Norton, one of the finest USMC pilots who soared above the clouds. Thank you all for your service.

Elaine Brye

To my son for following his passion to serve our great nation and helping me find joy in his journey. To my daughter who always knows how to keep me grounded in reality.

To America, land of the free and home of the brave for which I am forever grateful.

Army Mom Strong

CONTENTS

ACKNOWLEDGMENTS

A special thank you goes out to all the military moms we've met along the way, who have become kindred spirits on the best adventure ever!

Thank you to Tonya Brye of BryePhotography.com, who graciously let us use some of her beautiful photographs and even did a reshoot for the cover photo.

Thank you to Eric Brye for his badass photos as he takes flight. And thank you to Courtney Brye for his breathtaking photography that made its way into these pages.

Big thanks to my good friend Richard who meticulously read every word.

We are also grateful for the online communities that support military moms, without which we would never have met to work together on this book!

PREFACE

It's not easy to be a military mom. It is a life filled with big and small sacrifices, and a roller-coaster of emotions. Our journey begins the moment our children raised their hands and vowed to protect and defend.

When they made the brave and courageous decision to serve our great nation, the impact of that vow turned our lives around in ways we never imagined.

As military moms, we are all in this thing together.

Wherever we come from, whatever we do, we all share the same heart. We've met some amazing women along the way that also helped shape our journeys into a most positive experience.

Whether it is a physical hug or an online encounter, the bonds we have forged have made the path a little easier and the load a little lighter.

Through faith in God and confidence in our military children's abilities, we have learned to face our fears and find joy in this journey amid the emotional ups and downs.

We created this book to impart to you many of the lessons we learned to help you to stand strong in the face of fear and on the home front.

We must always remember that our children are part of the smartest and best trained military in the world. They are second to none. We love our children and our country. We are American military moms.

We hope you will gain some value, perspective, and inspiration from *The Heart of a Military Mom.*

God Bless you and your service member.

STRENGTH AND RESILIENCE
You Can Do This!

As my son was preparing to deploy to Afghanistan for a year, I felt myself slowly falling to pieces. Tears, sadness, and fear overwhelmed me on this journey to the unknown.

My mind was infused with the worst of the worst as I focused on the danger he would encounter in his job as helicopter pilot.

I had a decision to make.

I could spend the year of his deployment as a very upset parent crying much of the time, or I could decide to develop my inner strength and resilience.

I decided on the latter option. I gave myself a little time to transition through my sadness and fear before immersing myself in the necessary resources to help me find a way to be strong in the face of fear.

Spending a year sobbing my days away would not be of good service to anyone, especially me, not my family and certainly not my son.

So I started on my own journey to strengthen my heart, mind and soul, to learn how to face these challenges head on.

I started by embracing each step of my own journey as my son went along on his.

As a result, I emerged from that year stronger than I was before and helped hundreds of other military moms to find their own inner strength along the way.

With so many challenges faced by our military today, we must show our gratitude, honor them, and find ways to show our support. One important way that stands out in my mind is by keeping ourselves strong so we can continue to help make their mission possible.

This journey has been rewarding, life changing and a blessing.

I hope that you find some strength and resilience here.

Difficulties strengthen the mind, as labor does the body.
Lucius Annaeus Seneca

Some of us think holding on makes us strong; but sometimes it is letting go.

Hermann Hesse

During my son's first overseas assignment, I held on tight, too terrified to let go. I'm certain he felt my overbearing clinginess through countless phone calls and messages.

When I truly let go and realized our service members are well trained and competent, it was like a huge load lifted off me (and him!)

My confidence in them is what gives me strength, NOT hanging on.

We get stronger because it does not get easier.
Elaine Brye

Although proud of my son's choice, I was also fearful of the journey ahead. I was careful not to be that obstacle that got in his way.

Instead, I opted to support his decision no matter what. The second deployment is not much different than the first.

It is YOU that must be different. Your efforts to make a change can have a huge, positive impact on your daily life.

We just become more flexible and forgiving.

Semper Gumby!

We play an important role in supporting our service members. Staying healthy plays an important role in keeping us strong enough to continue this mission.

Army Mom Strong

As military moms, we are counted on to maintain stability, keep a sense of normalcy in the family, and be ready for whatever challenges come our way, especially during deployments.

Being prepared to carry heavy burdens also means being a healthy, powerful person.

Leading a healthy lifestyle keeps us moving in the right direction with our health, happiness, attitudes, mental outlook, and overall well-being.

Without these traits, it's hard to stand on one's own, never mind support someone else's mission!

Prescription for a Military Mom:
"Starve Fear and Feed Hope"

Elaine Brye

I work on this EVERY DAY. I squash the fears that rise up and focus on how brave and strong they are.

When my daughter had a surprise deployment to Afghanistan I was overwhelmed with fears.

I had to exercise my mind to focus on her competency and training. I imagined my fears being beaten back and looked forward to her homecoming and how much she was learning.

Starve fear and feed hope. It is my prescription for sanity.

I found strength in the fact that this career is my son's choice. It was his dream for a long time.

I always taught my children to pursue their passion and not let any obstacle get in their way. I was careful not to be that obstacle.

He was being true to himself and following his passion in life. For that I am so grateful.

My son is doing exactly what he always wanted to do. How many people can say that?

Not many that I know!

Do your duty.
Love your country.
Live with honor.
Suck it up.
Elaine Lowry Brye

When my dad went to Vietnam it was tough and a negative time in our country. No one thanked us for his service. Instead I was bullied at school and his service was derided.

But my mom was a smart woman. She empowered us with our family motto that helped us to be tougher together.

When the going gets tough I remember her words. We have a purpose. Back then it was to support my dad. Now it is to support my kids.

That motto, especially *suck it up*, has sustained me through my kids' twelve deployments.

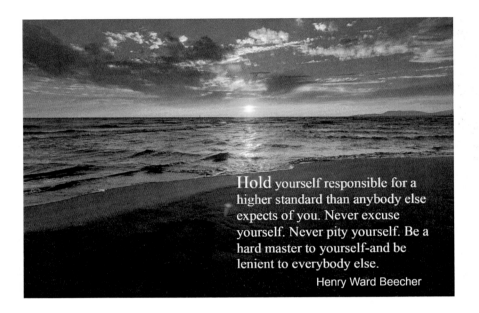

Hold yourself responsible for a higher standard than anybody else expects of you. Never excuse yourself. Never pity yourself. Be a hard master to yourself-and be lenient to everybody else.

Henry Ward Beecher

There is a time for baby days, and a time to let go of your adult children and allow them to soar.

When we see them as children who need to be protected, our fears and feeling of hopelessness increase.

We cannot do that anymore. It holds them back and holds us back.

We have to release them and allow them to fly. The same goes for us.

We need to soar with them.

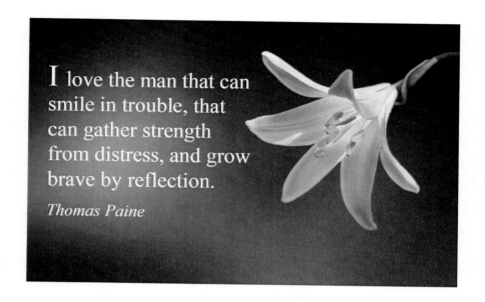

I love the man that can smile in trouble, that can gather strength from distress, and grow brave by reflection.

Thomas Paine

Every day I pray and look for new ways to cope with their absence and their duties. When I fill my heart with positive thoughts, stay busy, and seek joy, I feel stronger.

I choose not to give in to the fears and negativity that could easily take over.

We can become stronger with each new challenge.

We can survive the stress of the home front.

We must. Our children are counting on us.

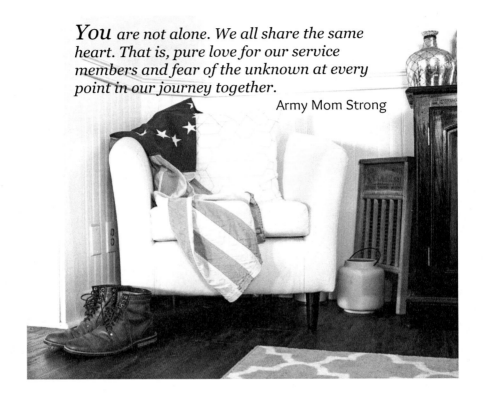

You are not alone. We all share the same heart. That is, pure love for our service members and fear of the unknown at every point in our journey together.

Army Mom Strong

We stand together linked by our common bond of love for our military children.

Wrap yourself up in the knowledge that you are not alone. We need to pool our strength and support to get through this journey of the unknown.

Reach out to another military mom just to let her know she is not alone and that you care.

Be strong and of good courage; be not afraid, neither be thou dismayed: for the Lord thy God is with thee whithersoever thou goest.   Joshua 1:9

As I watch my kids saddle up, I shout after them "Don't forget your spurs, your helmet ..."

As they ride off I bust out my saddle and ride the perimeter of the home front.

We all have our battles to fight.

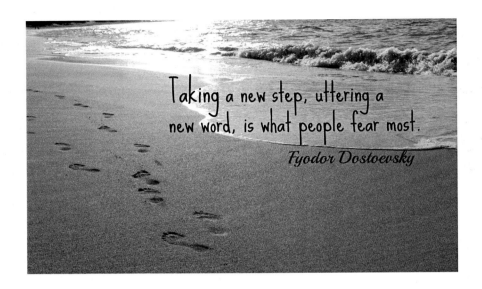

Taking a new step, uttering a new word, is what people fear most.

Fyodor Dostoevsky

When my son was at The Basic School for Marine officers they did increasingly longer ruck marches.

Loaded down with full gear, they plowed through the Virginia scrub and marshes for miles in the steaming heat.

Sometimes a platoon member crumbled unable to go on. They would be surrounded by fellow Marines, instructed to grab on, and they would be carried through the crisis of an uncooperative body.

The same goes for us. Somedays we just cannot do it anymore. Grab on. Repeat after me:

"March, left, right, left, right." Just keep moving forward.

The only way to deal with fear is to face it and push through it.

Elaine Brye

Fear is part of being a military mom.

Sometimes it is like a monster under the bed, hidden until you begin to rest. Suddenly it pops up, ready to overwhelm you.

Grab the flashlight and the broom. Sweep it away. Don't let it win your peace of mind.

It takes energy to fight it, but every time you win the battle of the mind you become stronger.

Practice being brave.

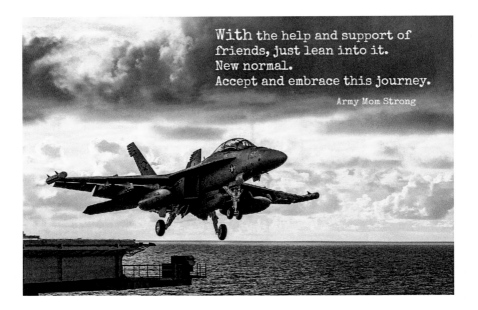

With the help and support of friends, just lean into it.
New normal.
Accept and embrace this journey.

Army Mom Strong

Deployment. After hearing that word one day, my heart sunk. Later that year, I'd be seeing my son off to a combat zone for a year.

Fear and sadness governed my life. That was unacceptable.

My son's service to our nation was not going to change, so I had to.

The best decision I ever made was to embrace and find joy in this journey, build my inner strength, and catch someone else when they fall.

WE ARE ALL IN THIS TOGETHER
You Are Not Alone

There was a period of about a dozen years when you would find me in the bleachers somewhere. My kids played almost every sport that was available and there I was rooting them on while I was developing a solid case of bleacher bottom.

I wish I had a dollar for every game or meet I sat through. But I did not need payment to be there. Many times I paid for the privilege to cheer for them, and support them.

It's what moms do.

But what about you Mom? Do you need someone encouraging you especially when you are learning to let go of your child to military service? How about when they are difficult places or in harm's way? Do you feel stressed or worried?

You are not alone.

Although you may feel alone at times, there are thousands of other moms who share this emotional journey with you. We know how it feels to stand there and watch your child walk away with a duffle bag of gear.

We know how it feels to be in a cone of silence when you wonder if they are ok, where they are and what they are doing.

How do you get to a place where you feel strong and brave? You practice it.

You constantly remind yourself of how capable and strong they are, and how you both have met every challenge so far. You remember how many other moms are standing in your shoes who understand. You focus on the positive and hang onto the thought that no news is good news.

We want to remind you that nothing has really changed from those days when you held down the bleachers. You are holding down your place on the home front, supporting and encouraging your military son and daughter.

We want to encourage you to be the strong mom you need to be, and that you have been since the day they were born.

You can do this!

As Military Moms, we share the greatest pride, the greatest fear, and the greatest faith - and we do this together. *Army Mom Strong*

When I found another military mom (who understood what I was feeling) to walk beside me and help me face my fears, my load got lighter.

We laugh. We cry. We pray. We worry. We listen to and support each other through the emotional ups and downs of this journey.

The military mom community goes beyond the boundaries of where you stand, broadening the area in which you can participate.

Lean into it together with open arms and keep moving forward, no matter where you are.

Face the challenge ahead.

Deployment day is coming. I must "lean into it" with open arms and keep moving forward.

Army Mom Strong

My son gave the best advice:

"Tell them that the United States has the most well trained Army in the world. We are professionals, all highly trained to do our jobs. Our military is second to none."

"We are confident and excel at our jobs. Tell them to have faith and confidence in what we do."

My son helped me be a little stronger that day.

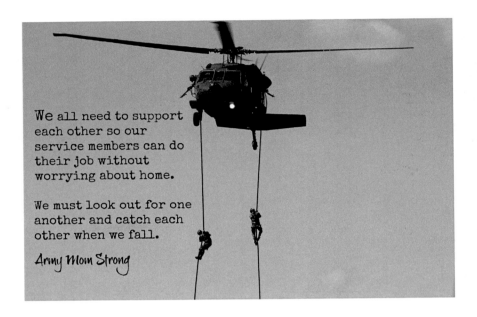

We all need to support each other so our service members can do their job without worrying about home.

We must look out for one another and catch each other when we fall.

Army Mom Strong

When my son headed to Air Assault School I had a lump in my throat. Who jumps out of a perfectly good helicopter? This made his tree climbing days look like a walk in the park! But he was well trained and had a team to work with. He was focused on the mission at hand.

I needed to lay low and not distract him with my concerns.

In the same way, we can be a team to hold each other up. As we lock arms we can become stronger so they don't need to worry about us.

We've got this!

We are all in this together.
Army Mom Strong

I marvel at our connection. When you stand and watch them walk away to war you feel a kinship to every other mom who ever stood in your shoes.

One day I saw a woman in the parking lot with Army Mom stickers all over her car. I approached her and introduced myself.

We held hands together in that moment with tears in our eyes as we spoke of our sons. She was a complete stranger to me but yet we understood each other completely in such a heartfelt and emotional moment.

We offered God's blessings to each other and went our separate ways.

Army "This We'll Defend"

Marine Corps "Semper Fidelis" (Always Faithful)

Navy "Non sibi sed patriae" (Not Self, but Country)

Air Force "Aim High ... Fly, Fight, Win"

Coast Guard "Semper Paratus" (Always Prepared)

THE HEART OF A MOTHER
When Duty Calls

Growing up as the oldest of seven, I was known as the second mom of my family. As a military kid, the frequent moves and my dad's deployments required me to step it up and help my mom. For a while I thought I would never have kids; I had wiped enough runny noses and changed dirty diapers for a lifetime. Then it hit, that biological time bomb that blew up in my heart. I wanted babies. I had some tough times with three miscarriages before I finally carried our oldest to term.

I really thought I knew what to expect as a mom, but when they laid that wrinkly slightly blue baby in my arms after 12 hours of labor I was overwhelmed. The love that swept over me also came with a mighty surge of adrenaline. I was a super hero. If I had to I am sure I could have lifted a car off that precious baby of mine. My love was not prissy, it was raw and primal, a grizzly bear kind of mother love. I would do anything to nurture and protect my child.

As the years went by my initial pregnancy issues were no more. I had three more babies in five years. Each time I was amazed that my mother love could grow and grow to encompass all of them. My days were spent training, educating, keeping them safe (which was not easy,) and doing laundry.

It was a full time job, especially as they got older.

I wanted them to soar, to reach their full potential and "be all they could be." As they became young adults each one came to me with their future decision. They wanted to join the military. Part of my divided heart swelled up with pride. The other part, the one that wanted to keep them safe, filled with fear. I would be giving them up to their country's service and my role would diminish. It was heartbreaking and glorious at the same time. They were on the path to becoming their best self.

I had to focus on that thought.

Now the initial days of saying goodbye are over. I have learned to say goodbye over and over again, to watch them soar high in the sky with a fireball propelling them or rotors pushing them up in the heavens. They are responsible for many other mothers' children. I marvel at their skills as they do the work of warriors. But my grizzly bear momma heart would have me putting on body armor and toting a weapon right beside them if I could. Instead I stay behind on the home front, fighting battles for them here and supporting them in every way I can.

I am a military mom who loves them wherever duty calls. That's the heart of a mother.

No language can express the power and beauty and heroism of a mother's love.

Edwin Chapin

Love reckons hours for months, and days for years; and every little absence is an age.

John Dryden

Saying goodbye to our child is hard enough without knowing they are heading for a dangerous vocation.

Waiting for that first phone call is almost unbearable.

I spoke with a mom who just dropped her son off for basic training.

"It's just like labor, keep breathing." In and out. Just keep breathing. Its good practice for those harder goodbyes when it seems like time stands still.

Just keep breathing.

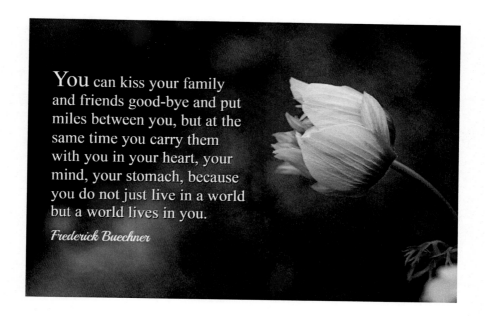

You can kiss your family and friends good-bye and put miles between you, but at the same time you carry them with you in your heart, your mind, your stomach, because you do not just live in a world but a world lives in you.

Frederick Buechner

My service member is always in my heart and on my mind.

Sometimes I can handle it; sometimes I cannot which results in quiet tears. When sadness overwhelms you, let those moments be moments, and then get on with enjoying your life.

It's not right to forfeit your happiness and not fair for your loved one to shoulder the burden of being the cause.

It's not about avoiding these feelings; instead, it's about managing those feelings so they do not govern your day-to-day life.

Faith consists in believing when it is beyond the power of reason to believe. *Voltaire*

When my son is halfway around the world, it's easy to fall into that anxious, worried state of mind. Too many sleepless nights with my mobile phone close-by taught me a good lesson.

Anxiety tears you down and faith builds you up. I chose faith so I can also help support and build up others, including my children.

Making the right choice is crucial to whether we feel depressed, sick and unable to focus, or feel uplifted, energized, and ready to conquer whatever the day has in store.

Garner up pleasant thoughts in your mind, for pleasant thoughts make pleasant lives.
John Wilkins

Sweet memories of dandelion bouquets from earnest preschool faces merge with the steely faced warriors you have become.

I hold onto those memories of younger carefree days when service responsibilities get challenging, and deployments just keep coming.

You are always on my mind and in my heart.

To be prepared for war is one of the most effectual means of preserving peace.

George Washington

Try as we might, nothing but a hug from your child will fill the emptiness we feel in our heart when our child is in harm's way.

Upon seeing my son off for deployment, I hugged him tighter than I ever did before. There are some moments in life that you never forget and this was surely one of them.

We hugged for a long time as I told him the only words I could get out with emotions welled up inside me, "*stay safe – I love you.*"

A hero is one who knows how to hang on one minute longer.

Novalis

I marvel that this is the same kid who was afraid of monsters in the night and now fights darkness in the world.

He is still the same fun loving, silly and smart young man. But he also knows how to shoot a gun, drop bombs from an aircraft, and fight for our freedom as he rides into this adventure.

This kid grew up to be a highly trained man, ready to do the really hard stuff.

I look fear in the face to find joy in the journey.

Don't be afraid, for I am with you. Don't be discouraged, for I am your God. I will strengthen you and help you. I will hold you up with my victorious right hand.

Isiah 41:10

A MOTHER'S PRIDE

Honor their Calling

When people learn that I have four children serving in the military they always ask: "How do you cope?"

I employ an assortment of strategies. Staying busy, working on projects, and taking care of myself are all part of my tool kit to survive life as a military mom.

Above all else, faith is my bed rock, with pride just beside it. It is not a "my kid is better than your kid" kind of pride. Instead, it is rocket fuel for my soul that sustains me.

What do I mean by that? Let me take you back to when they were little. We were so excited when they spoke their first words or took their first steps. I saw my job as a mother to be teaching and encouraging them to be become their best.

It began with those first steps and evolved into teaching them to navigate a bigger world. Those first steps onto the school bus led to more challenges and teaching opportunities. We rejoiced when they learned to read, began to understand the world around them, and could have meaningful conversations with us.

There were also lessons in character and ethics. The concepts of responsibility and honor had to be explained and modeled. The importance of doing the right thing, following through, and caring about others were an integral part of that education process as they grew.

When each child came to me and said they had decided to join the military, my heart was divided. The primordial response was fear, "What if something happens to you?"

In an unstable world we do need those who are willing to stand and fight, and put it all on the line to protect our freedoms. I was overwhelmed that they chose to be that volunteer to sacrifice self for us all.

As I watch them train and become proficient in their military jobs I continue to hang onto that sense of awe and thankfulness. My children are part of a force for good.

In fearful times they have the watch. They continue to pursue excellence and we can count on them.

I am so very proud of what they do and who they have become.

In times of turbulence hang onto to that pride. Our children have set themselves apart by their devotion to duty, honor, and country.

Let that pride wash over you and protect you from the anxieties that can seem overwhelming at times.

What would we and our country do without them?

The true soldier fights not because he hates what is in front of him, but because he loves what is behind him.

G.K. Chesterton

I am greatly obliged to you, and to all who have come forward at the call of their country.

Abraham Lincoln

Where does it come from, the desire to face any challenge to make this country a better place?

Our kids have committed to step up and serve whether it is on angry seas or faraway deserts.

Every one of us benefits from their selflessness. I am just amazed at their courage and strength.

It reminds me that I need to do my part to make our country a good place with a strong home front.

They need us behind them cheering them on.

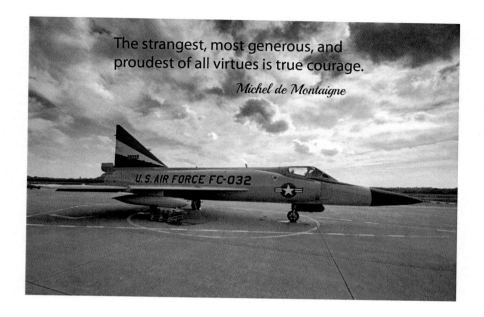

The strangest, most generous, and proudest of all virtues is true courage.

Michel de Montaigne

When I watch my sons climb into their cockpits and soar into the sky I fight the urge to yell "Get back down here, that's too scary!"

I need to strap in and push through the fear.

It beats curling up in the fetal position (believe me, I've done it.)

I am proud that it is my child who is willing to protect us all; despite the personal risks they take to keep us safe. It's not every day that you meet people who will do this type of job, but my son does and I am darn proud of him.

Other moms I know speak proudly about their kids, as they should: Johnny is a big shot at a company, Sally is a vet - oh, the animals are just so cute, and Sam owns his own small business. My son drops 500-pound bombs as he flies high supporting the best of the best in Afghanistan!

How's that for a conversation stopper!

I never truly realized how blessed I was to be an American until I spent a year teaching in Afghanistan. I saw women suffer without the basic freedoms I was used to.

The ravages of war had taken its toll on everyone and I saw first-hand why our children's deployments there mattered.

Freedom is not a gift. It must be fought for, sometimes at great cost. We must support those who fight those battles for all of us.

This nation will remain the land of the free only so long as it is the home of the brave.

Elmer Davis

My heart is broken every time I say good bye.

That's when thoughts of *"Will I ever see them again"* flicker in my mind. I have to hold on to the hope that they will return safely and the knowledge that they are the heroes of our time.

We need them to be willing to protect and defend this beloved country of ours.

As they sail away it especially helps me when I remember what and who they are fighting for.

Discipline is the soul of an army. It makes small numbers formidable; procures success to the weak, and esteem to all.

George Washington

My son has been through some really grueling training: Survival, Evasion, Resistance, and Escape also known as SERE. My first reaction was *Oh no! How will he get through this?*

My next reaction was "Thank God he is going through this!" He is prepared and at the ready for whatever comes his way in a combat situation.

Difficult military training is the foundation for the courage, commitment, and discipline that is needed to be a defender of freedom.

I am so proud to be the Mom of a defender of freedom!

If you enjoyed "The Heart of a Military Mom," you'll love

Finding Passion and Purpose While Your Loved One Serves

Coming in Fall 2017

Follow the link below to sign up for notification about the book.

HeartofaMilitaryMom.com/passion

YOU KNOW YOU'RE A MILITARY MOM

A Mission of Determination

When my son made a courageous and determined decision to start his career with the Army, I was oblivious to military matters. I didn't understand much of what he was telling me in military speak and acronyms.

I remember when he left for Basic Combat Training. I cried at the airport and frankly didn't know what to expect. I even called the military base at some point.

I don't recommend doing that!

Maybe I just needed to hear a voice that was in that world because I was not.

Life went on as usual. Then I visited my son during Advanced Individual Training (AIT). It was during the Fourth of July. We went to a military base where there was a huge celebration with music and fireworks.

I knew I was a military mom the moment the National Anthem was played.

Sitting at the water's edge, there were military service members all around us, patriotic music playing and tears streaming down my face.

A few years later, when my son was in Afghanistan, I attended a business conference. I'll never forget standing in the back of a huge auditorium holding onto my phone for dear life!

It was the only place in the room where I could get a cell service signal. What if he called? I was not going to miss it.

There was no mistaken that I was a military mom. I felt different than every other person in the room. Who else would have stood like that for hours?

Over the years, I have visited my son around the world and stateside. The first time I found myself in an airport noticing men and women in uniform, the tears started again. I was so choked up I could barely thank them for their service, or speak a word. I was surely a military mom.

As time passed, I knew every Army helicopter and their mission, had grandkids that knew how to salute, and could spot another military parent from across a parking lot.

I had arrived. I knew I was a military mom.

Regardless of the emotional roller coaster, I wouldn't have it any other way.

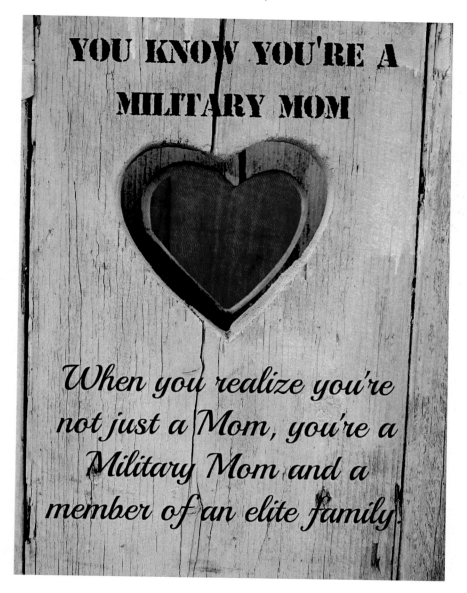

YOU KNOW YOU'RE A MILITARY MOM

When you realize you're not just a Mom, you're a Military Mom and a member of an elite family.

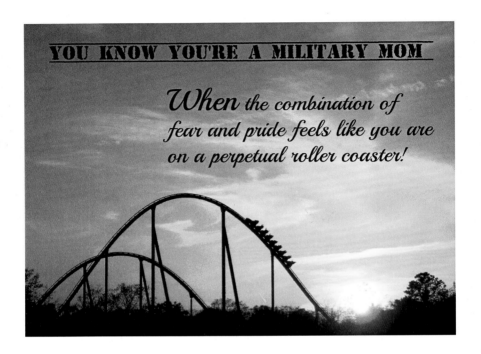

YOU KNOW YOU'RE A MILITARY MOM

When the combination of fear and pride feels like you are on a perpetual roller coaster!

The roller coaster ride is real. One minute I'm immersed in enjoying all that life has to offer, and the next my heart is filled with the fear of the unknown. That's when the tears start!

I'm in awe of how easily I can shift from one emotion to the next without conscious effort.

In these times I remember to accept and move through my emotions, and use my strengths to feel energized and empowered.

My personal mission is to handle these fears without losing a sense of well-being.

You Know You're a Military Mom

When your phone never leaves your side, even when sleeping.

My connection used to be an umbilical cord, now it is a mobile phone.

I remember the one time I left my phone at home while running an errand. After having a near panic attack, I turned my car around and headed home to grab it. *It never happened again.*

My phone became the master key that unlocks the door to knowing my son is safe and sound.

Every call and every text is a proof of life I need to keep sane and hopeful.

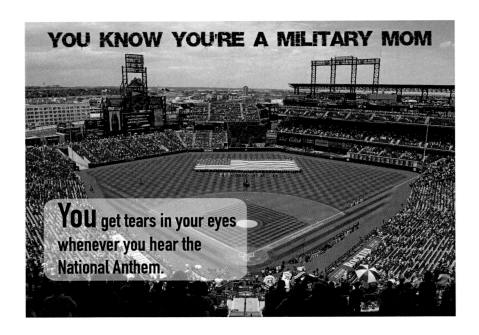

YOU KNOW YOU'RE A MILITARY MOM

You get tears in your eyes whenever you hear the National Anthem.

I was a new military mom and we were heading to a baseball game.

As we stood for the National Anthem the tears came out of nowhere. I was ambushed. As the tears flowed I tried to hold back the sobs.

Now I am ready for it. I start out singing bravely but always lose it at the Rocket's Red Glare! By the time we reach "home of the brave," I am undone.

My countdown until we reunite starts the minute they leave my side.

They do dangerous work, travel to difficult places, and much of the time they cannot tell me anything about it.

I cannot think about saying goodbye, but only look forward to when I see them again

I have to believe I will see them again.

From the rivers of Afghanistan to the sands of Okinawa, our children serve with integrity and bravery.

They make us proud wherever they are.

When my first child joined the military, Afghanistan was just a name on a map.

Now it has become their address for multiple years. We never know where their paths of duty may lead.

YOU KNOW YOU'RE A MILITARY MOM

When you suddenly deal with fears you never knew existed.

I remember suddenly being assaulted by a wave of fear that I had never considered before.

Sometimes I long for the simple life I had when life was smaller. But here we are.

It has been a difficult road, wrapping my mind around the job that my son loves, wherever and whenever duty calls.

The more I learn and face the fear, the more I can appreciate and find joy in his love for this mission.

Accept, embrace, and lean into it.

You Know You're a Military Mom
Your last good night of sleep was several months before your loved one deployed.

Sometimes I don't know what is worse: The insomnia or the bad dreams that sneak in from my worried subconscious.

But I do like to hope that my kids are sleeping soundly. I will stay awake for all of us.

It's no mystery that the day my son returned from his deployment, I slept like a baby for the first time in a year. It felt amazing!

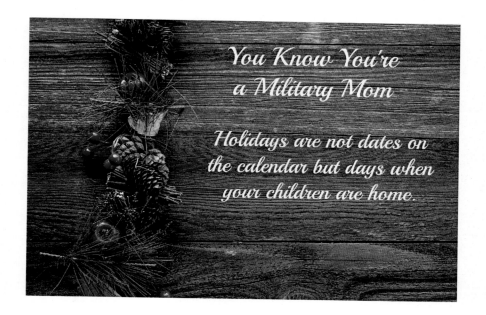

You Know You're
a Military Mom

Holidays are not dates on
the calendar but days when
your children are home.

It was early November. A small Christmas tree sat in the corner of the room with colored lights, decorative ornaments, and small children squealing with delight at the sparkle and joy.

You could not mistake that our family was celebrating Christmas, with presents under the tree and a turkey dinner with all the trimmings.

If you see Christmas cheer a little too early at someone's home, they may be sending a loved one off to a military deployment.

Keep them in your prayers and let them know they are not alone.

YOU KNOW YOU'RE A MILITARY MOM

When boots on the ground might have your children wearing them.

When I hear the phrase, "Boots on the ground" bandied about by politicians and news anchors I cringe.

Our troops are sons and daughters, mothers and fathers, husbands and wives who have committed their lives to serve our country. They will do their duty and follow orders but they are so much more than boots on the ground.

They make me proud every day.

People wonder why I have my cell phone on at all times, even in church. I will drop everything to answer it even if it is an unknown number.

Just hearing their voice makes my day, my week, and my month. It is proof of life that fills my heart.

For that moment I know all is well and that makes all the difference.

You Know You're a Military Mom

When you suddenly realize that you made it through the tough times and emerged as a stronger more resilient person.

My most challenging assignment in life was working on my inner self through my son's first deployment. Looking back over that year, I got to choose which direction I was pulled into.

Like a magnet, negativity and sad emotions could have easily pulled me down into a deep darkness.

Instead, I focused on what type of person I wanted to be at the end of that deployment and let that be the stronger pull.

Everything we achieve is not by accident. It's a matter of making a decision and becoming more than we are to handle every step along this journey.

YOU KNOW YOU'RE A MILITARY MOM

Embrace the suck becomes your words to live by.

Embrace the suck. What does that mean? Our sons and daughters know all too well. They learned it in Basic Training.

It means lean in to the hard things and push past them. Don't stop to whine or complain. The only thing that is going to help is to grab-on.

It's the same for us. We don't need to waste time and energy in pity parties. They have a mission to complete and so do we. Ours is to support them whatever way we can.

We cannot afford to get mired in the muck. We are on duty too.

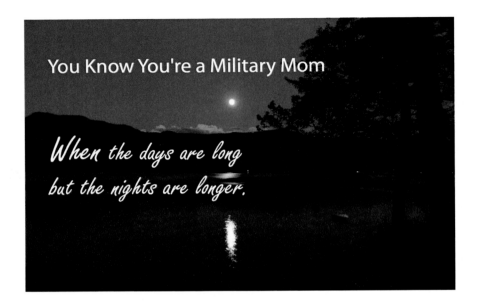

You Know You're a Military Mom

When the days are long but the nights are longer.

Now I lay me down to sleep and my subconscious battle takes over. Although I keep up a stiff upper lip throughout the day the fears begin to betray my seemingly calm exterior.

I have not slept through the night since my first son joined in 2001. Knowing they are in harm's way makes it hard to keep the anxiety at bay all day.

It's like having a newborn but much scarier.

I say my prayers, think positive thoughts, and have my battle buddies on speed dial in case I need a pep talk at 2 AM. It's just what we military moms do to make it through the night.

You Know You're a Military Mom

When your two-year old
Granddaughter knows how to salute.

It was a special day. My mother, Army Veteran, Army wife, military mom, and grandmother, was being laid to rest at Arlington National Cemetery with full military honors.

As we stood for "Taps" and the final goodbye, I looked over to see my granddaughter saluting. She was following the lead of her mommy and daddy, both Air Force service members and her uncles representing the Army, Navy, and Marines. She was born into a family with a legacy of service and has learned the lesson at this young age.

Duty, Honor, Courage, Commitment, and Love of Country are words to live and grow by.

CONNECTIONS

We hope you find these resources helpful.

Heart of a Military Mom helps military moms face fears through value, perspective, and inspiration.

HeartofaMilitaryMom.com
Facebook.com/heartofamilitarymom

Army Mom Strong provides support, resources and prayer to moms, dads, siblings, and other family of Army service members.

ArmyMomStrong.com
Facebook.com/armymomstrong

Be Safe, Love Mom supports and connects those who love and support their military children. Her website is based on the philosophy of her acclaimed book, "Be Safe, Love Mom."

BeSafeLoveMom.com
Facebook.com/besafelovemom

ABOUT THE AUTHORS

When Lisa's son prepared for a deployment, she shed many tears amid sleepless nights. Feeling alone and unprepared, she scoured the Internet to educate herself about the mission over there, in a strange mix of fear and pride. Her search led her to found Army Mom Strong, an online Facebook community of over 93,000 that supports moms of Army service members.

Over the years, she learned to find joy in this journey whether it be deployments, or overseas and stateside duty assignments, while strengthening her inner resolve.

She is fiercely dedicated to her family and enjoys traveling the globe for frequent visits with her family, wherever they may be. She is an avid runner, passionate about living a healthy lifestyle and helps others do the same through natural solutions.

Her adventures as an Army Mom over the past 13 years led her to create "The Heart of a Military Mom" to help inspire others who embark on this journey.

Elaine Lowry Brye is a mom who knows about letting go. Like many moms, she cried when her kids left home, wishes they'd call and write more, and spends sleepless nights worrying about them. But Elaine's tears and concerns are even more poignant than most mothers'— because Elaine is the mom of four military officers, one each in the Air Force, Army, Navy, and Marines.

An Army brat turned ROTC candidate turned military wife, Elaine never expected her kids to have a call to serve, and certainly didn't expect all four to join up. Three of her kids—two sons and a daughter—attended the Naval Academy, and it was there that Elaine got her own calling: she joined the Naval Academy Parents' Listserv, and began a sixteen-year journey of helping moms and dads adjust to their strange, new, lonely lives as military parents. She also spent a year teaching in Kabul, Afghanistan where she experienced life in a war zone. Her love of her country and desire to support her fellow parents led to her to write *Be Safe, Love Mom: A Military Moms Stories of Courage, Comfort, and Surviving Life on the Homefront* and created BeSafeLoveMom.com to further support and connect those who love their military children.

"Do your duty, love your country, live with honor and suck it up" is her mantra as she encourages military moms to face the challenges and struggles of military life with courage. She hopes the lessons learned in "The Heart of a Military Mom" will be empowering and inspirational and provide a reminder that we are not alone in our love, worry and pride for our beloved children.

50200240R00042

Made in the USA
San Bernardino, CA
27 August 2019